Ode To The Road

Dr. Alveda King

Ode To The Road
© 2024 Dr. Alveda King

ISBN 9798991931106

JEC Publishing
3645 Marketplace Blvd
Suite 130-592
Atlanta, GA 30344

This book is dedicated in gratitude to God
for His infinite love, grace and mercy;
and to faithful road warriors everywhere.

KEEP LOOKING UP!

Psalm 121:1

Long ago...

A kind knight came along today
It's happened once or thrice
A damsel in distress was I
Indeed about to cry

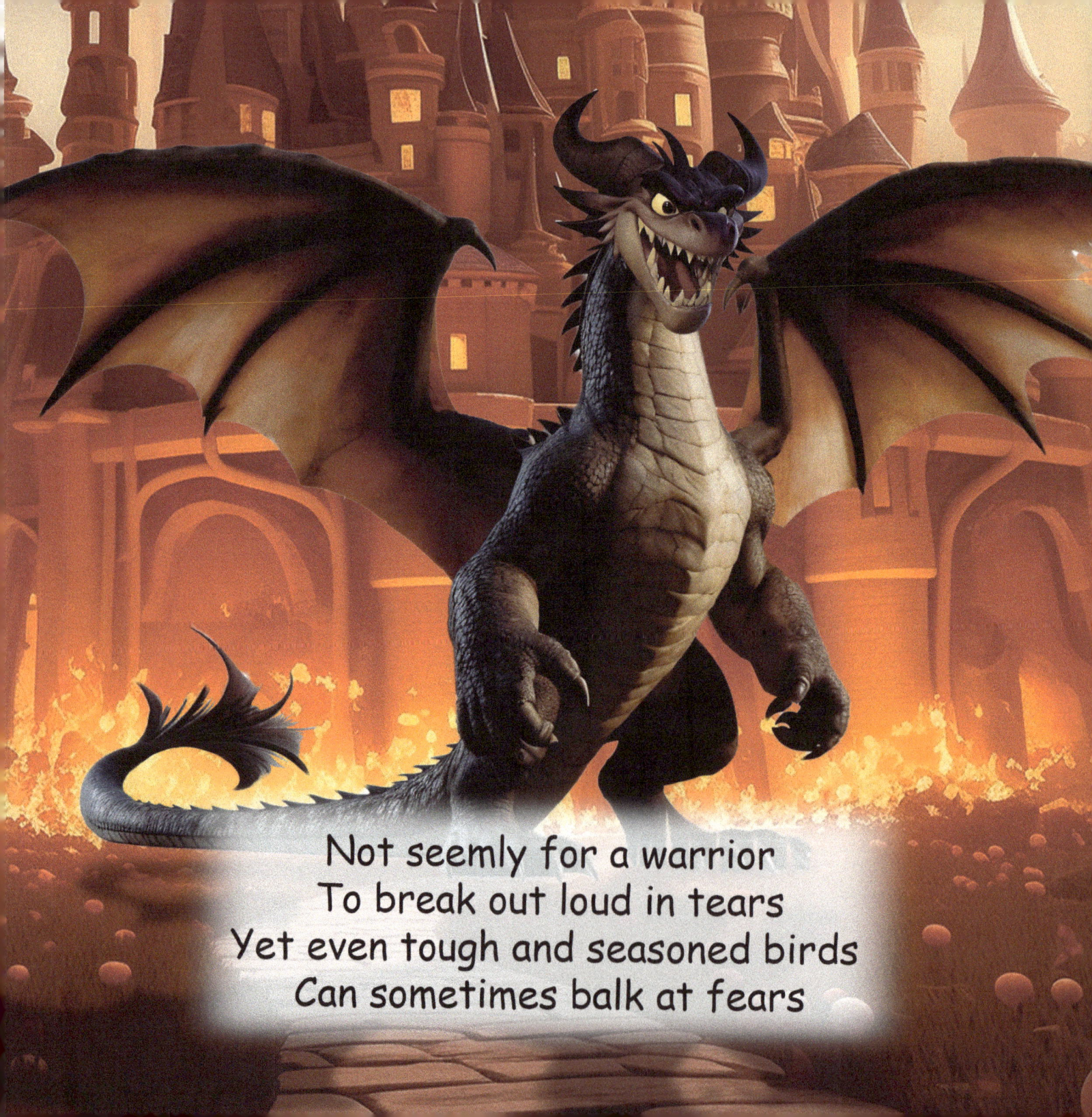

Not seemly for a warrior
To break out loud in tears
Yet even tough and seasoned birds
Can sometimes balk at fears

Years later..

This is how the story goes
Always from the road
With heavy bags and aching limbs
And burdened by the load

I travel many trails for God
Too often sans a friend
Yet sometimes God sends a soul
To help go round the bend

ATLANTA

Once long ago...

Out on the road
I faced a tiny jam
Was out alone and out of sorts
And praying for a tram

Then a shiny limousine appeared
An answer to my plight

As "Can I help you ma'am?"
Made things again alright

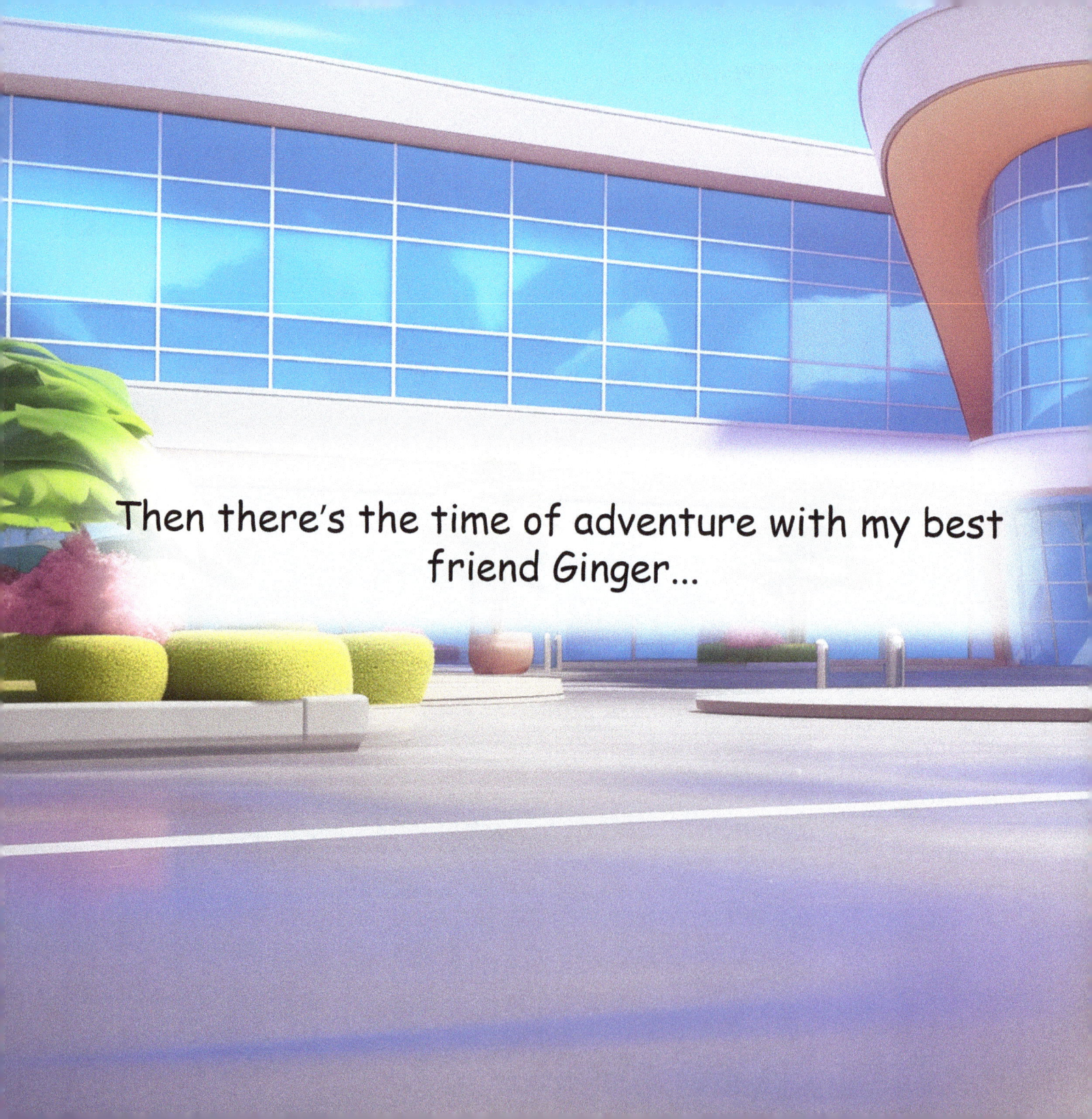

Then there's the time of adventure with my best friend Ginger...

With double bags and double struggle
We wrestled with bag dolly
How we ended up this way
We wondered "oh my golly"

Then we heard a chuckle
From a gallant passerby

Stepping up he used his foot for balance
Gracious my oh my

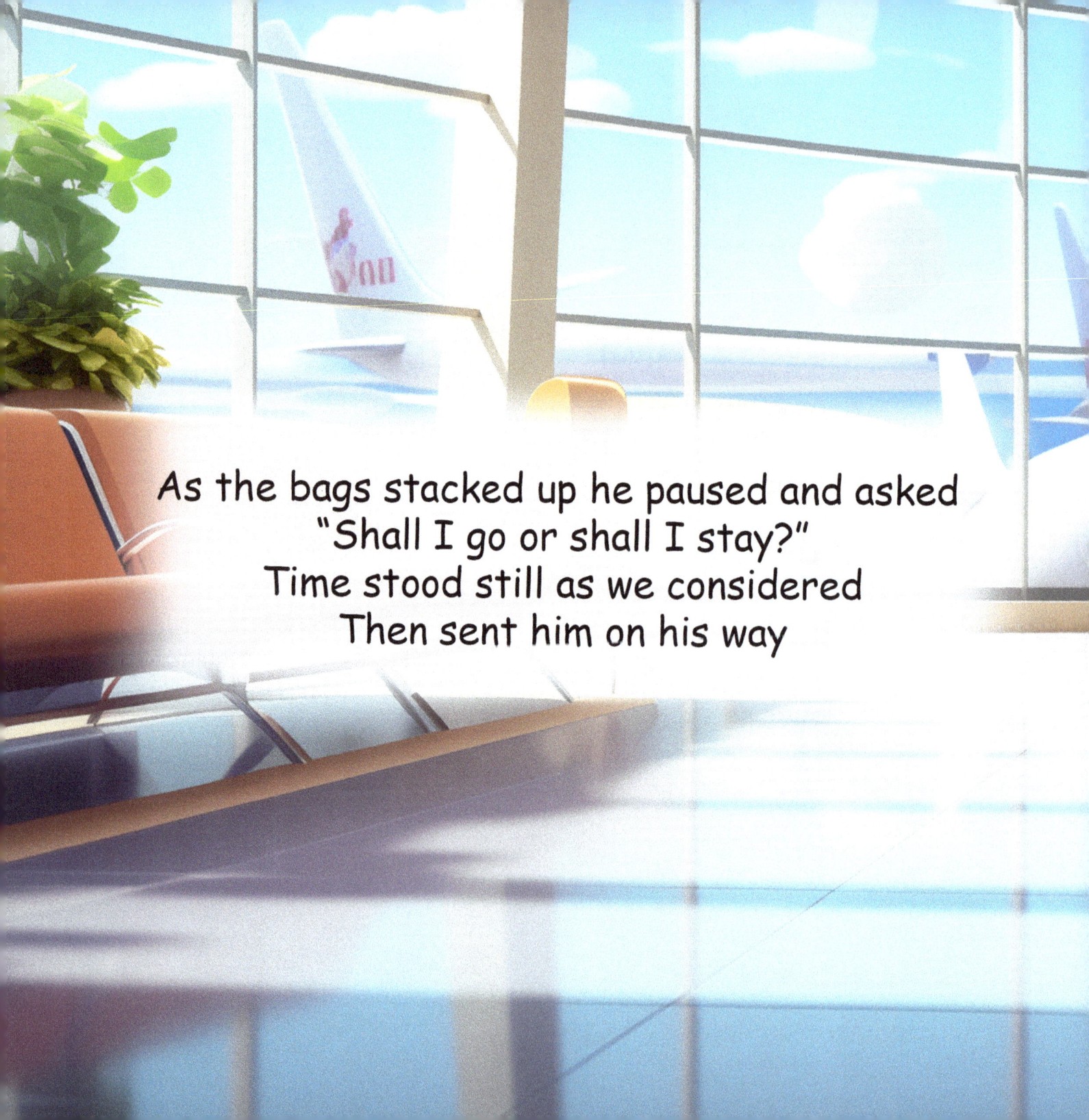

As the bags stacked up he paused and asked
"Shall I go or shall I stay?"
Time stood still as we considered
Then sent him on his way

Ginger said "Hey that's a song!"
And we all smiled and laughed
Then rolled along to finish strong
Oh what a day we had

And then...

To top it off I made my plane
And on the ramp I met
Another soul who cleared my path
And peaceful flight was set

Thevisiontvshow.com

So God today I pray with thanks
That chivalry's not dead
And bless those souls along the road
Who offer love instead
Amen

Dr. Alveda King

Evangelist Alveda C. King, PhD is Chair of the AFPI Center for the American Dream. She is a guardian of The King Family Legacy, and is a graduate of Aidan University. She is the founder of Alveda King Ministries (www.alvedaking.com (http://www.alvedaking.com/)) and co-founder of She Leads Georgia and Speak for Life. Alveda is also an acclaimed author, television host, blog contributor and co-producer of The Vision TV Show. Alveda was twice elected to the Georgia State House, a presidential appointee, the recipient of the Presidential Lifetime Achievement Award, Senior Advisor at Priests for Life, Senior Advisor Coral Ridge Ministries, Founder of King Legacy Farms, a lifetime member of Cooking Club of America and Optimist International, a former college professor and school principal ; and is a film and music veteran.

Dr. Ginger Howard

Faith in God and fashion unite in the success and beauty of Ginger Howard. As Alveda's co-author of WE'RE NOT COLORBLIND, and owner of a delightful boutique Ginger Howard Selections, in Buckhead, Ginger is passionate about the importance of modesty and beauty of "lady-like" styles, both of which guide her selections for the fashion-forward clothes available at her store; and to the young ladies she mentors.

Eartha Sims, Extraordinaire

With a gift and talent for generating creative ideas and organizing shows, "Miss Eartha" brings joy to life in the performing arts. Her extensive professional training includes studies and degrees from Spelman College; Opera/Theatre/Dance Kennesaw State University; and Joel Katz Music B.A. in Theatre Performance Studies. With her poetic, lyrical and dramatic writing and performance skills, her songs and stage presence often glorify God and inspire audiences.

Dr. Celeste Beal

With degrees in French, Psychology and post graduate Law, as well as travels abroad to teach English as a second language in Europe, with years of experience as a motivational speaker while working as an ESOL professor, Celeste rounds out her goals by administering peace and justice. Celeste currently serves as a Small Business Consultant. She is also a certified trainer in the Philosophy and Methodology Of Nonviolence at the Martin Luther King Center in Atlanta Georgia.

Bria Edwards, Millennial Influencer

Bria Edwards is an accomplished digital strategist and media expert with a proven track record of blending innovative content creation with strategic communications to drive organizational success. Her career began as a journalist, evolving into a social media influencer and corporate events planner, where she has consistently excelled in shaping brand narratives and increasing engagement.

alvedaking.com

Ode To The Road Lyric Video

Ode To The Road Video